the **TINY BOOK** of

SCRIPTURES

for **INDIVIDUALS** with

SCHIZOPHRENIA

LISA LACON, PH.D., CRC

LUCIDBOOKS

The Tiny Book of Scriptures for Individuals with Schizophrenia
Copyright © 2024 by Lisa LaCon, Ph.D., CRC

Published by Lucid Books in Houston, TX
www.LucidBooks.com

Unless otherwise indicated, scripture quotations are taken from the (NIV) the Holy Bible, New International Version®, NIV®. Copyright ©1973, 1978, 1984, 2011 by Biblica, Inc.™ Used by permission of Zondervan. All rights reserved worldwide. www. zondervan.com The "NIV" and "New International Version" are trademarks registered in the United States Patent and Trademark Office by Biblica, Inc.™

Scripture quotations marked (NLT) are taken from the Holy Bible, New Living Translation, copyright ©1996, 2004, 2015 by Tyndale House Foundation. Used by permission of Tyndale House Publishers, Carol Stream, Illinois 60188. All rights reserved.

ISBN: 978-1-63296-710-7
eISBN: 978-1-63296-712-1

Special Sales: Most Lucid Books titles are available in special quantity discounts. Custom imprinting or excerpting can also be done to fit special needs. Contact Lucid Books at Info@LucidBooks.com

DEDICATION

To Jen, wherever you are.

CONTENTS

Schizophrenia is a serious mental illness that affects how a person thinks, feels, and behaves. People with schizophrenia may appear to have lost touch with reality, which can be distressing for them, and their family, and friends. This book is in no way meant to offer medical advice or treatment for schizophrenia. If you have, or believe you have, or know a loved one you believe has schizophrenia, please seek treatment from a qualified medical professional.

"The Tiny Book of Scriptures for Individuals with Schizophrenia" is a tool filled with scriptures to assist in combating some positive symptoms of schizophrenia (hallucinations and delusions) by helping individuals distinguish between the voice of mental illness versus the voice of God.

AUTHOR'S NOTE

Know that you are deeply cherished by the Lord, thy God referenced in Genesis 1:1, the Creator of this universe. Your diagnosis does not define your essence; it is merely one aspect of your being. As someone grappling with schizophrenia, you may confront a myriad of questions, such as "Why me?" or "What is happening to me?" While these inquiries are valid, satisfactory answers may remain elusive. Instead of fixating on these uncertainties, let's take a proactive approach and concentrate on strategies to alleviate symptoms. This handbook is tailored for individuals contending with positive symptoms of schizophrenia, specifically hallucinations and paranoid delusions.

Hallucinations, as defined by the DSM-5, are "perception-like experiences that occur without an external stimulus" (American Psychiatric Association, 2013, p. 87). For instance, you may hear voices or see individuals that others do not. Essentially, these experiences create a disconnect from reality because the perceived entities lack objective existence.

Delusions, as per the DSM-5, are "fixed beliefs that are not amenable in light of conflicting evidence" (American Psychiatric Association, 2013, p. 87). In simpler terms, your belief system regarding certain people, places, or things is flawed and remains unchanged despite contradictory evidence.

Unchecked hallucinations and delusions are considered "psychotic." The Mayo Clinic defines psychotic as a "mental disorder marked by a detachment from reality" (Mayo Clinic, 2024, April 5).

This disconnection from reality often contributes to underemployment, unemployment, homelessness, and high mortality rates among individuals diagnosed with schizophrenia. These mortality rates can be categorized into two groups: self-harm and/or harm to others.

Because of this phenomenon, various tools are employed to mitigate the adverse impacts of schizophrenia. For instance, evidence-based practices such as supportive housing and supported employment aid individuals with schizophrenia in achieving a sense of normalcy in their lives.

Another valuable resource is the Word of God. It's important to note that while the Word of God can offer support, it should not replace seeking assistance from a medical professional. However, it can be a beneficial addition to your recovery journey.

Why is the Word of God essential in reducing harm for individuals with schizophrenia?

According to Hebrews 4:12, the Word of God is "quick, and powerful, and sharper than any two-edged sword, piercing even to the dividing asunder of soul and spirit, and of the joints and marrow, and is a discerner of the thoughts and intents of the heart."

This means the Word of God can discern between truth versus deceit. The reality is that individuals who aren't managing their symptoms of schizophrenia are being deceived. There are instances of individuals with schizophrenia who believe they are being instructed by God to inflict harm upon themselves or others (*God told me to kill...*). Being able to differentiate between the voice of mental illness and the voice of God can indeed help individuals in preserving their own lives and the lives of others.

"The Tiny Book of Scriptures for Individuals with Schizophrenia" is divided into three sections. Section 1 contains scriptures that can provide comfort during moments of self-harm ideation: *(God told me I need to kill myself; I think I need to jump off this building, etc.).* Section 2 features scriptures for managing thoughts of harming others: *(God told me to rob this store; God told me to kill my child who is possessed by the devil, etc.).* Finally, Section 3 includes scriptures to combat fear-based thoughts: *(There are people trying to kill me. I must hide).* When reading from this Tiny Book, reflect on His Word. Whenever harmful thoughts arise toward yourself or others, or when anxiety and fear grip you, immerse yourself in these scriptures. Read them out loud or to yourself until you internalize and believe the truth conveyed by the Word about you and about His love toward you.

Let this mind be in you, which was also in Christ Jesus: who, being in the form of God, thought it not robbery to be equal with God: but made himself of no reputation, and took upon him the form of a servant, and was made in the likeness of men.

Philippians 2:5-7

SECTION 1

SCRIPTURES TO COMBAT HARMING YOURSELF

For I know the plans I have for you,"
declares the LORD, "plans to prosper
you and not to harm you, plans to give
you hope and a future. Then you will
call on me and come and pray to me,
and I will listen to you. You will seek
me and find me when you seek me
with all your heart.

Jeremiah 29:11-13

The thief comes only to steal and kill and destroy; I (The Lord) have come that they may have life and have it to the full.

John 10:10

I praise you because I am fearfully and wonderfully made; your works are wonderful, I know that full well.

Psalm 139:14

For we are God's handiwork, created in Christ Jesus to do good works, which God prepared in advance for us to do.

Ephesians 2:12

PRAYERFUL CONFESSION

Dear Lord God, I know You have plans for me to prosper and for me not to harm myself. I know the thief comes to steal, kill, and destroy. I know that You came to give me life and life more abundantly. I know that I am made by Your handiwork and because of that, I am wonderfully made. And no weapon formed against me will prosper. I know I can do all things through Christ who strengthens me. I say this prayer in the name of the Lord Jesus Christ. Amen. So let it be.

SECTION 2

SCRIPTURES TO COMBAT HARMING OTHERS

Do not judge, and you will not be judged. Do not condemn, and you will not be condemned. Forgive, and you will be forgiven.

Luke 6:37

Get rid of all bitterness, rage, and anger, brawling and slander, along with every form of malice.

Ephesians 4:31

But I tell you, love your enemies and pray for those who persecute you.

Matthew 5:44

Love is patient, love is kind. It does not envy, it does not boast, it is not proud. It does not dishonor others, it is not self-seeking, it is not easily angered, it keeps no record of wrongs. Love does not delight in evil but rejoices with the truth. It always protects, always trusts, always hopes, always perseveres.

1 Corinthians 13:4-7

PRAYERFUL CONFESSION

Dear Lord God, I know Your Word says for me not to judge and not to condemn others. I pray You give me the spirit of discernment to know the difference between Your Word versus the word of something else. Please Lord remove all bitterness, rage, and anger from my mind and my heart. Let me focus on loving those who may not love me and pray for them who use me. I say this prayer in the name of the Lord Jesus Christ. Amen. So let it be.

SECTION 3

SCRIPTURES TO COMBAT FEAR

For God has not given us *(me)** a spirit
of fear and timidity, but of power, love,
and self-discipline.

2 Timothy 1:7 NLT
* added word

Do not be anxious about anything, but in every situation, by prayer and petition, with thanksgiving, present your requests to God.

Philippians 4:6

When I am afraid, I put my trust in you. In God, whose word I praise—in God I trust and am not afraid. What can mere mortals do to me?

Psalm 56:3-4

So do not fear, for I am with you; do not be dismayed, for I am your God. I will strengthen you and help you; I will uphold you with my righteous right hand.

Isaiah 41:10

PRAYERFUL CONFESSION

Dear Father God, I know You love me and will never allow fear to take over my life. You said for me not to be anxious about anything, but to put my trust in You. I will not fear because I know You are with me, and that You will never leave me nor forsake me. I put my trust in You and not man. I will not be afraid. I say this prayer in the name of the Lord Jesus Christ. Amen. So let it be.

REFERENCES

American Psychiatric Association. (2013). Schizophrenia spectrum and other psychotic disorders. In *Diagnostic and statistical manual of mental disorders* (5th ed., text rev.).

Mayo Foundation for Medical Education and Research. (2022, December 13). Mental illness. Mayo Clinic. https://www.mayoclinic.org/diseases-conditions/mental-illness/diagnosis-treatment/drc-20374974

ABOUT THE AUTHOR

Dr. Lisa LaCon is Co-Founder and Director of BLESSED Ministries, Inc., a nonprofit workforce development organization. She holds a Ph.D. in Psychiatric Rehabilitation from Rutgers University and a certification as a Rehabilitation Counselor. In addition, she is the Founder and Executive Producer of Urban Tools for Change Network, her YouTube channel, for residents who live in the urban community who would like to know more about mental health issues and how to achieve wellness and recovery goals.

www.ingramcontent.com/pod-product-compliance
Lightning Source LLC
LaVergne TN
LVHW052341080426
835508LV00045B/3339